Need to Know

Painkillers and Tranquillizers

Michael Durham

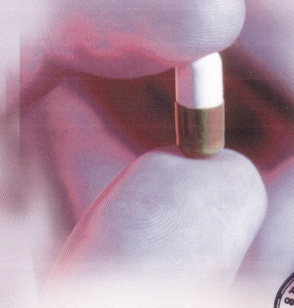

Heinemann
LIBRARY

www.heinemann.co.uk/library

Visit our website to find out more information about **Heinemann Library** books.

To order:

 Phone 44 (0) 1865 888066

 Send a fax to 44 (0) 1865 314091

 Visit the Heinemann Bookshop at www.heinemann.co.uk/library to browse our catalogue and order online.

Produced by Roger Coote Publishing
Gissing's Farm, Fressingfield, Suffolk IP21 5SH, UK

First published in Great Britain by Heinemann Library, Halley Court, Jordan Hill, Oxford OX2 8EJ, part of Harcourt Education.
Heinemann is a registered trademark of Harcourt Education Ltd.

Editorial: Cath Senker
Design: Jane Hawkins
Picture Research: Lynda Lines
Production: Viv Hichens

Originated by Ambassador Litho Ltd
Printed and bound in China by South China Printing Company

ISBN 0 431 09811 5
07 06 05 04 03
10 9 8 7 6 5 4 3 2 1

British Library Cataloguing in Publication Data
Durham, Michael
  Painkillers and tranquillizers. - (Need to know)
  1.Medication abuse - Juvenile literature
  2.Analgesics - Juvenile literature
  3.Antidepressants - Juvenile literature
  I.Title II. Parker, Steve
  362.2'99

Acknowledgements
The publishers would like to thank the following for permission to reproduce photographs:
Corbis *front cover (girl)* (Helen King), pp. 7 (Jose Luis Pelaz), 8 (Bettmann), 9 (Bettmann), 23 (Helen King), 24 (LWA/Stephen Welstead), 47 (Robert Huntzinger), 48 (David Woods); Sally and Richard Greenhill p. 15; David Hoffmann Photo Library pp. 13, 17 top; Photodisc *front cover (pills)*; Popperfoto pp. 17 bottom (Reuters), 30 (Reuters); Rex Features pp. 36 (Nils Jorgensen), 39 (Sierakowski/SEN), 44 (Isopress Senepart/SEN), 49 (SIPA); Science Photo Library pp. 1 (BSIP/PIKO), 4 (Damien Lovegrove), 10–11 (Adam Hart-Davis), 28 (CC Studio), 32 (Damien Lovegrove), 37 (Arthur Trees), 38 (BSIP/PIKO), 40 (CC Studio), 41 (Oscar Burriel), 43 (Oscar Burriel), 46 (Oscar Burriel); Topham pp. 12 (Image Works/Bob Daemmrich), 18 (Image Works), 21 (Image Works), 25 (Image Works/Bob Daemmrich), 27 (Image Works/Arlene Collins), 29 (Image Works/Nancy Richmond), 35 (Image Works), 51.

Every effort has been made to contact copyright holders of any material reproduced in this book. Any omissions will be rectified in subsequent printings if notice is given to the publishers.

Any words appearing in the text in bold, **like this**, are explained in the Glossary.

Contents

Painkillers and tranquillizers

Painkillers and tranquillizers are among the most widely used of all medical drugs. Since the dawn of time, people have tried to ease their pain by taking potions and powders. Perhaps more recently, they have used various substances to try to stay calm in the face of anxiety and worry. Advances in modern science have brought powerful ways of achieving these ends. Medicines that lessen aches and pains are sold in grocery stores and corner shops. Doctors can prescribe pills that help to reduce cares and worries and bring a more peaceful life – for a time.

Obtaining the drugs

Some painkillers, usually the less powerful types, are available **over-the-counter** (OTC). This means they can be obtained without a doctor's prescription, usually from a pharmacist (chemist) or from a general store. Other painkillers, generally the stronger versions, are available only from a pharmacy, with a doctor's prescription. Tranquillizers are obtained mainly by prescription. However, both groups of drugs sometimes make their appearance 'on the street' as part of the illegal drugs trade.

Both painkillers and tranquillizers are available in a wide range of types and strengths. These are known by various names, including the chemical name of the drug, and also the trade or brand name that is used by the drug manufacturer. The variety of names can be extremely confusing.

The dangers

Drugs such as painkillers and tranquillizers have brought huge benefits to many people. But, like other medicinal substances, they can also cause unwanted effects and problems.

One problem is **overdose**. An overdose of any drug is harmful, but with some painkillers it can be deadly. Another problem is **dependence**. This is an especially high risk with certain tranquillizers. Also, painkillers and tranquillizers can interact with each other, or with other drugs such as alcohol, to threaten both physical and mental health. In rare cases, the result may be fatal.

People taking painkillers or tranquillizers should take great care, as with any drug. This applies both to prescribed and over-the-counter types. Sometimes a person may worry that any benefit of the drug will be outweighed by **side effects**. A pharmacist or doctor can give information about such matters. There may be a range of 'non-drug' choices for dealing with the person's difficulties, such as a change of lifestyle, counselling or a **complementary therapy**.

What are painkillers and tranquillizers?

Painkillers or pain-relievers are also called **analgesics**. They help to reduce or ease pain, although they may not get rid of it entirely. Some types, like **aspirin** and **paracetamol** (known in the USA as Tylenol), are available without a doctor's prescription. This is because they are well established and relatively safe. They are used to treat common ailments such as backache, headache and toothache. But if they are taken at the wrong dose, then like any drug, they can be dangerous. They may also have **side effects** in certain people.

More powerful painkillers

Stronger painkillers can only be obtained with a doctor's prescription. Most contain **morphine**, or morphine-like substances. Morphine is a natural substance from certain kinds of poppy flowers. Most of these stronger morphine-type painkillers are known scientifically as **opiates** or **opioids**. (This group of drugs also includes **heroin** and **opium**.) Under supervision of a doctor, they may be used for someone recovering from an operation in hospital, or for a person suffering from a serious, painful illness such as cancer or arthritis.

Morphine-based painkillers can be extremely dangerous. They have various side effects and the user risks **dependence** – needing to keep taking them. So they are **controlled drugs**, which means they can only be prescribed and possessed with special permission.

Tranquillizers

Tranquillizers alter people's moods. They are usually prescribed for a short period by a doctor. These drugs are for people suffering from great anxiety, worry, nervousness or sleeplessness. Most tranquillizers have a calming or **sedative** effect (they make people feel sleepy). They help people to feel less worried, upset and agitated, and more positive and able to cope with life. Some types reduce extreme 'highs and lows' of emotion.

In general, tranquillizers work quickly and last for a few hours, occasionally longer. Someone who feels particularly anxious or agitated could take a tranquillizer and start feeling the benefits almost straight away. This is why these drugs can help people to get to sleep.

The history of painkillers

Before modern scientific medicine, people used natural substances they found around them to treat illness and ease pain. In particular, certain kinds of plant leaves, flowers, stems and roots have been used through the ages, for their medicinal qualities. Some of these natural medicines, if used wrongly, were dangerous or even deadly. But others proved remarkably effective, and many of the synthetic (man-made) drugs available today are based on them.

In 'opium dens' people used the saps and juices of certain poppies to alter their mood and awareness.

The first painkillers

The first doctors were shamans or priests. They used rituals such as chanting and dancing, and also natural medicines, to treat the sick and relieve pain. The powerful natural painkiller **opium** has been known for thousands of years. Other medicinal plants that can have pain-reducing effects include ginseng, Siberian wort, mandragora, hemlock and willow bark.

However, these types of natural painkillers were often unreliable, difficult to use, and sometimes dangerous. In some cases they hardly seemed to work at all. In other cases, a person could accidentally be given an **overdose**, and suffer severe **side effects** or even die. In the 1800s, one of the most common painkillers was laudanum, which was made from opium and alcohol. But many people became dependent on it. Another traditional way to relieve pain, for example during an operation, was to give patients large amounts of alcohol. This helped to dull pain. In fact, it often did far more, and made the patient so drunk that he or she fell asleep and felt nothing.

Pain during operations

Pain relief during operations was controlled better in the late 19th century. Doctors and dentists began to use gases, such as ether and chloroform, to put their patients to sleep during surgery. Today there are many kinds of **anaesthetics** that reduce feeling and pain.

Aspirin was the first painkiller suitable for general use by people with common aches and pains. It was put on sale by the Swiss company Bayer in 1899, as 'the wonder drug that works wonders'. In fact, aspirin is one of the oldest painkillers. The chemical that has the painkilling effect is known as salicylate. It is found in the bark of certain trees, such as willow. Its pain-relieving qualities have been known for 2500 years.

"Pain is inevitable; suffering is optional."

(A traditional saying that means we all suffer pain, but the way we deal with it, and the amount of suffering it causes, are more individual matters.)

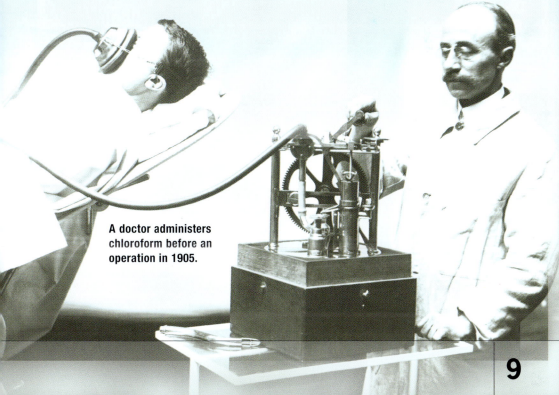

A doctor administers chloroform before an operation in 1905.

The history of tranquillizers

For thousands of years people have used natural substances to alter their mood and make them feel more contented. Alcohol can have this effect, acting to calm an agitated person. Substances were also extracted from coca leaves and **opium** poppies for their mind-altering qualities.

Many herbal plants have been used as natural remedies for anxiety, and to help people sleep. They include valerian root and camomile tea. These and others were used for people who 'suffered from nerves' or who were 'highly strung'. Such natural medicines were also used by people who had '**nervous breakdowns**'. Many of these herbs are still used today.

The modern era

The first modern tranquillizer made by chemical methods was chlordiazepoxide. It was developed by chemist Leo Sternbach in 1957. Tests showed it had a **sedative** and calming effect. It was marketed in 1960 as **Librium**, and soon became one of the biggest-selling medicines in the world.

Chlordiazepoxide belongs to a group of tranquillizers called **benzodiazepines** or 'benzos'. Its discovery led to the development of other tranquillizers in the group. One is diazepam, stronger than Librium and marketed as **Valium**. Another is nitrazepam, with the trade name **Mogadon**; it works more quickly.

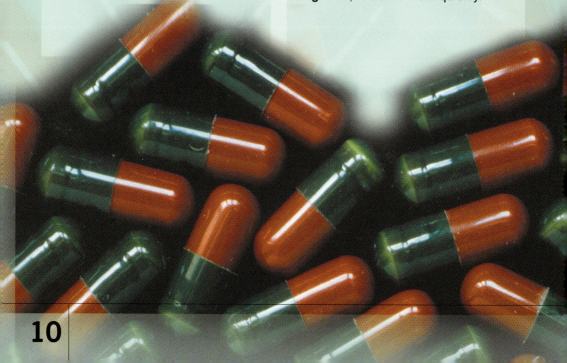

'Happy pills'

During the 1960s and 1970s, benzodiazepine tranquillizers were hailed as safe, effective pills for a wide range of problems, especially the stresses and strains of daily living. They gained nicknames such as 'happy pills' and 'mother's little helpers'. This was because they were often prescribed for mothers with young children, coping with hard lives.

A drug company advert aimed at doctors showed such a mother pinned inside a 'prison' of brooms and mops. The slogan was 'You can't set her free, but you can help her feel less anxious'. However, as the prescriptions for benzodiazepines increased, so did the problems they caused, especially **dependence** (see page 38).

> **❝She goes running for the shelter,**
> **Of a mother's little helper,**
> **And it helps her on her way,**
> **Gets her through her busy day.❞**

(From *Mother's Little Helper*, a song about benzodiazepines by The Rolling Stones, 1967)

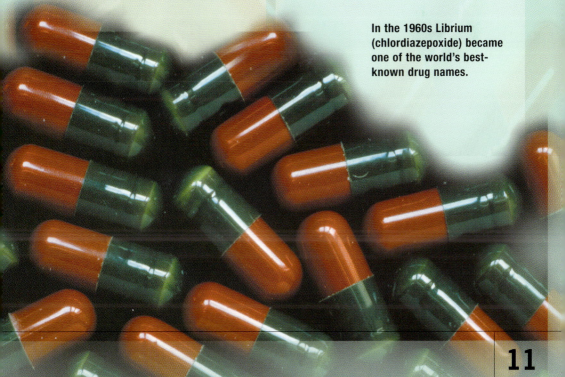

In the 1960s Librium (chlordiazepoxide) became one of the world's best-known drug names.

What is pain?

You are the only person who can feel your pain. This makes describing a pain difficult. We use words such as 'sharp', 'hot', 'stabbing', 'shooting' or 'dull'. But how do we know that we are all using these descriptions in the same way? Also, when does a slight ache, twinge or discomfort become a real pain? If several people had exactly the same painful condition, would they all feel the same type and amount of pain? There is no scientific method of comparing the amount or severity of pain between different people.

Inside the body, pain exists as a series of tiny electrical signals called nerve impulses. These are made by tiny nerve endings known as pain sensors, usually when damage has been caused to a body part, after a hard knock, for example. The signals travel along nerves to the brain. The person becomes aware of them in his or her mind, as a painful sensation.

Types of pain

- A sharp, sudden pain, for example when you stub your toe, is sometimes called protective pain. It is a reaction to danger, like an early warning system.
- The throbbing, longer-lasting pain that sets in after a more serious injury is called reparative pain. It means damage is being repaired.
- Neuropathic pain is a severe, long-term pain as a result of damage to the nervous system itself.

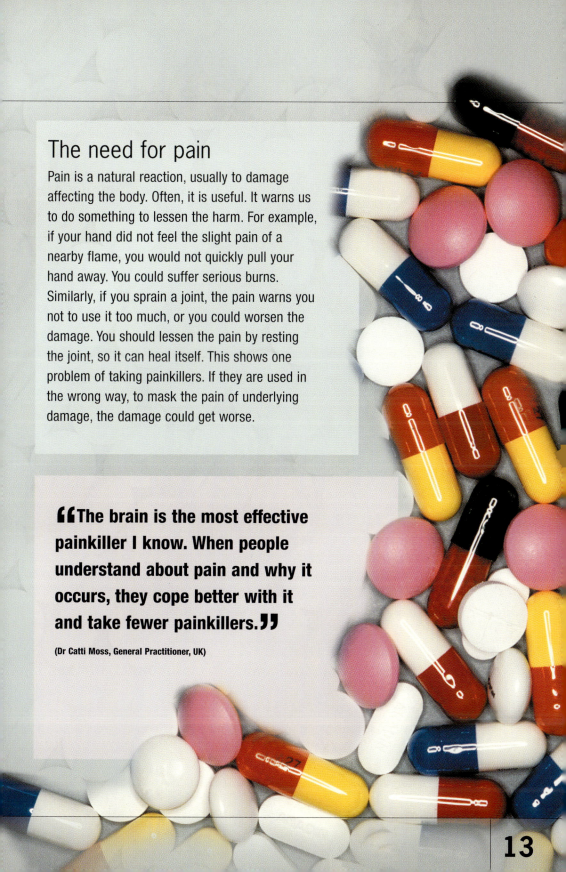

The need for pain

Pain is a natural reaction, usually to damage affecting the body. Often, it is useful. It warns us to do something to lessen the harm. For example, if your hand did not feel the slight pain of a nearby flame, you would not quickly pull your hand away. You could suffer serious burns. Similarly, if you sprain a joint, the pain warns you not to use it too much, or you could worsen the damage. You should lessen the pain by resting the joint, so it can heal itself. This shows one problem of taking painkillers. If they are used in the wrong way, to mask the pain of underlying damage, the damage could get worse.

❝The brain is the most effective painkiller I know. When people understand about pain and why it occurs, they cope better with it and take fewer painkillers.❞

(Dr Catti Moss, General Practitioner, UK)

How do painkillers work?

Painkillers do not kill pain by removing the cause of it. If someone suffers a hard knock on the arm, then the area is painful. There might be swelling and a bruise. If that person takes a painkiller, the pain lessens. But the damage, swelling and bruising are still there. Only as the area heals and repairs itself, does the cause of the pain fade away.

Stopping pain signals

Most painkillers interfere with the way that the signals for pain pass along the body's nerves, or change how the brain deals with the signals.

Some types of painkiller affect the pain sensors that detect damage and produce the signals in the first place. Other painkillers dampen down the signals as they travel along nerves to the brain. In both these cases, the signals do not reach the brain itself.

The other main group of painkillers work on the brain itself. The nerve signals from a painful area reach the brain. But then they are altered or blocked. This affects the way the sensation of pain is recognized and 'felt' in the mind.

Anti-inflammatories

Some painkillers, such as **aspirin**, relieve pain in other ways too. They are **anti-inflammatory**. This means they reduce the swelling, redness, heat and soreness of inflammation, where the body is suffering damage. Other painkillers work in different ways to aspirin. All these differences show the importance of matching the type of painkiller to the nature and cause of the pain.

Julie's story

Julie, 14, suffered from severe menstrual (period) pains that lasted two or three days. After a talk with her family doctor, she tried changes in her diet and her lifestyle, including exercises. The problem lessened but still caused discomfort. At the next visit, the doctor suggested a prescription painkiller. However, Julie did not want to be tied to a strong prescribed drug, which she felt might cause long-term problems. So the doctor suggested further changes in lifestyle, especially in diet and coping with stress. She said that Julie could try taking **ibuprofen** a day before her period was due, if necessary. Julie can now get on with her life much better, and she doesn't need to visit the doctor regularly for a prescription.

Types of painkiller

Aspirin is a common painkiller. It reduces pain in several ways. One is by stopping the production of natural body chemicals called prostaglandins. These are made in any body part that is injured or damaged. Normally, their job is to 'announce' that damage has occurred. They affect the pain sensors, so that they send signals to the brain. If prostaglandins cannot be made, the messages are not sent, and the person does not feel pain. Aspirin also helps to reduce inflammation in joints and muscles. The inflammation itself causes pain, so reducing it lessens the pain.

NSAIDs

Aspirin is known as a non-steroidal **anti-inflammatory** drug **(NSAID).** **Ibuprofen** (called Nurofen in the UK and Australia, Advil in the USA) is another NSAID and works in a similar way. NSAIDs are often prescribed for painful, long-term conditions such as arthritis, neck pain or backache, where keeping down inflammation is also important. (There is another large group of drugs known as steroids, which also act against inflammation. But steroids are very different in chemical form to NSAIDs, and work in different ways.)

Paracetamol

The most common **over-the-counter** painkiller is **paracetamol** (called Tylenol in the USA). It relieves pain and, like aspirin, it also reduces fever and brings down body temperature. Paracetamol has few **side effects**, and usually it is safe for both adults and children. But unlike NSAIDs such as aspirin, paracetamol does not have anti-inflammatory effects. Also, it is extremely dangerous if an **overdose** is taken (see page 19).

Powerful painkillers

The group of powerful painkillers called **opiate-opioids** includes **morphine**, pethidine, methadone and **heroin**. These drugs are sometimes called **narcotic analgesics** because they can bring on narcosis (sleep so deep that it becomes unconsciousness). Most carry serious risks, especially **dependence**. Their use is therefore closely controlled, and doctors can only prescribe them in carefully monitored cases, such as for seriously ill hospital patients.

The business of growing poppies to produce drugs such as morphine and heroin still occurs, even though it is illegal in most places.

Powerful morphine-based painkillers enter the body in small, measured amounts, along a tube or drip.

Morphine and heroin are sometimes given to people with very painful, long-term medical conditions. Pethidine may be given to women as a form of pain relief during childbirth. The only over-the-counter opiate is **codeine**, which is sometimes mixed in tiny quantities with aspirin, ibuprofen or paracetamol.

Side effects of painkillers

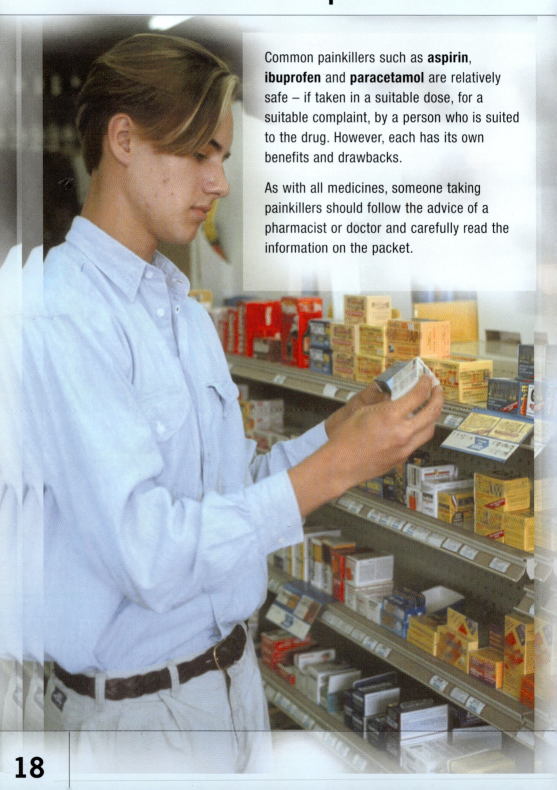

Common painkillers such as **aspirin**, **ibuprofen** and **paracetamol** are relatively safe – if taken in a suitable dose, for a suitable complaint, by a person who is suited to the drug. However, each has its own benefits and drawbacks.

As with all medicines, someone taking painkillers should follow the advice of a pharmacist or doctor and carefully read the information on the packet.

Most drugs have **side effects**. This is especially true of drugs that alter the workings of the brain and nervous system. So, while the drug seems to solve one problem, it can be creating another. Some pills also react dangerously with other medicines and even with common foods and drinks.

Stomach bleeding

The most serious side effect of **over-the-counter NSAID** painkillers such as aspirin and ibuprofen is the risk of stomach bleeding. The drug attaches itself to important chemicals in the stomach, called enzymes, and prevents them from working. Every year a number of people become ill, and a few may die, after taking NSAID painkillers. The risk is small (fewer than 1 person in 10,000 each year in the UK), but significant. Figures for one year in the USA (late 1990s) show that the side effects and other effects of aspirin and other NSAIDs resulted in 16,500 deaths, chiefly due to bleeding in the stomach and gut. Such NSAIDs are not recommended for people who have suffered stomach ulcers or similar stomach problems in the past.

Dangers of aspirin

Aspirin should not be taken by people at risk of kidney or liver problems. Also, it is dangerous when mixed with alcohol. There have been claims that taking aspirin or ibuprofen can make it more likely for a pregnant woman to have a miscarriage (lose her baby). Usually the painkiller paracetamol is more suitable for a woman expecting a baby, if she really needs to take a painkiller at all.

Aspirin is not recommended for children under 12 years. Paracetamol can be used by children in small doses, and in general, it has fewer side effects than NSAIDs. But paracetamol has its own drawbacks. A major problem is the danger of an **overdose**, accidental or deliberate. It is possible to take a fatal overdose of any painkiller, but paracetamol is especially risky because it damages the liver very quickly. Unless immediate action is taken (within six to eight hours), this damage cannot be reversed. It may well lead to a slow and painful death.

Why do people need tranquillizers?

Everybody feels anxious, agitated, worried or upset at some time. People have problems such as passing exams, getting on with their family, finding a job, making friends, or losing a partner or close relative. Most of the time, we recover from these feelings naturally. After a while, new events and situations come along, and life looks more positive and fulfilling again.

Constant worry

But for some people, worry and nervousness do not always have a particular cause. They have anxious feelings most of the time, often for no specific reason. They feel fearful and jumpy, and lack confidence. Even if things are going well, they worry in case things go wrong. They may expect the worst, all the time.

In a few people, these feelings of anxiety, agitation and worry become so powerful, and last so long, that they take over daily life. The person can no longer carry on as normal. The anxiety affects sleeping and eating, home and work, and relationships with family and friends. It may begin to affect the person's health too, so that he or she begins to suffer from infections and illnesses.

Drug treatment

If this stage is reached, a doctor may advise that treatment with a tranquillizer drug could help. The aim of the anti-anxiety drug treatment is to provide a breathing space. It enables the person to lose the agitation, worry and nervousness, and get back towards calm confidence and positive thoughts. It is like a 'push-start' in the right direction. Gradually the person can return to a more normal lifestyle. Hopefully, the drug will be needed for a short while only and after a few weeks the patient can stop taking it.

❝We have doctors, nurses, teachers, judges and TV personalities among our clients. If you tried to sell them cannabis on a street corner, they'd be horrified. But many of them have stressful jobs, and these drugs make them feel calmer.❞

(David Greive, founder of Over-Count, an organization that helps people to beat dependence on OTC drugs, 2000)

Anxiety may seem similar to **depression** (see page 29). Both can involve feelings of sadness and a lack of confidence. However, there are differences between anxiety and depression, and in the drugs used to treat them.

Stress can be dangerous. Young children often demand constant attention, which can cause great stress. This can affect a person's judgement, such as allowing children too close to a cooker.

Why do people need tranquillizers?

Almost anybody can be prescribed a tranquillizer, if a doctor feels anxiety and worry are severe, disabling and causing the person unacceptable distress. Almost anyone, in any area of life, may be prescribed them – shop workers, professors, teachers, retired train-drivers, astronauts and bricklayers. Everyone gets anxious now and then, of course. But it would be very unusual for a doctor to suggest tranquillizer drugs straight away, without trying other courses of action.

For example, a tranquillizer would not help a young person at school with 'exam nerves'. It could seriously affect memory and ability to concentrate, and bring on feelings of being less alert and more tired. Often, with this type of worry, a talk with a teacher, counsellor or trusted adviser can help. An older person may worry about being forced to retire early. Again, there are other courses of action, including advice and training in new skills.

Women and men

Medical research shows that women are three times more likely to be prescribed tranquillizers than men. Nobody is quite certain why.

One suggestion is that doctors may be more likely to suggest tranquillizers to women, compared to men. Another theory is that men cope with stress and worry by bottling it up inside or pretending it is not important, so they are less likely to visit a doctor with this problem. Women are more likely to visit a doctor because they realize something is wrong and want to get it out into the open and deal with it as soon as possible.

However, research into **dependency** problems caused by tranquillizers can show a different picture. In one project, three times more men than women with tranquillizer habits were seen. Many of the men did not obtain their tranquillizers on prescription, but

“Whatever the diagnosis – Librium.”

(Drug company advert from the 1970s)

from the illegal drugs trade. They tended to use both tranquillizers and alcohol as a form of escape, to 'get away from it all' for a short time. Most women, on the other hand, had been prescribed tranquillizers for anxiety or stress. But the prescriptions had continued for too long and they had become dependent on them.

Types of tranquillizer

Tranquillizers work in various ways. Some have an effect in a few hours, while others are slower to act. Each drug has different features and should be selected by the doctor to suit each patient's needs.

Benzodiazepines

Most tranquillizers belong to a drug group called **benzodiazepines**, or 'benzos'. There are two main types. The **hypnotic** types work quickly but last only a few hours. They include nitrazepam (**Mogadon**) and **temazepam**. These are sometimes used to treat 'panic attacks', when great anxiety comes on rapidly, perhaps started by a small event that quickly grows into a tremendous worry.

The **anxiolytic** types include diazepam (**Valium**) and chlordiazepoxide (**Librium**). Their effects take longer, but last longer too.

Benzodiazepines are sometimes called 'minor tranquillizers'. They produce feelings of calm and relaxation. Most also tend to make people feel sleepy, and they may be prescribed as sleeping pills.

Benzodiazepines tend to act on the parts of the brain involved in anxiety, but rarely on other parts. They should not alter a person's general behaviour. However, some do affect other parts of the brain, and so have other uses – for example, to control epilepsy.

Barbiturates

Barbiturates are powerful tranquillizer drugs, rarely used today. **Dependence** on barbiturates occurs easily, and giving them up causes serious **withdrawal symptoms**. Also the danger of a fatal **overdose** is high.

Barbiturates cause serious **tolerance** and dependence problems, comparable with those of 'hard' drugs such as **heroin**. These problems are rare because barbiturates are strictly controlled. They are used medically only in rare cases, such as to control severe epilepsy. Also, as drugs of abuse, they have largely been replaced by other substances that users say give a stronger effect and which have fewer immediate **side effects**.

Sean's story

Sean, 16, went to his doctor complaining that he could not sleep and always felt agitated and worried. His doctor suggested the feelings would pass and discussed positive new interests with Sean and his parents. But Sean's anxiety did not go away. So the doctor, with reluctance, prescribed seven tablets of a mild tranquillizer. Sean could take one if he felt particularly bad.

At the same time, the doctor arranged for Sean to see a psychologist (an expert on the mind and behaviour). This showed the real reasons for Sean's anxiety. He was being bullied at school, and he had also recently broken up with a girlfriend. After these reasons had come into the open, Sean realized he did not need the pills. He managed to change school and gradually made new friends.

Side effects of tranquillizers

A common **side effect** of tranquillizers is a feeling of 'flatness' or 'greyness'. A person may feel the anxiety and worry lessen. But he or she may now be thinking more slowly, be less alert and aware, and more confused and drowsy. These are known as **sedative** effects.

Tranquillizers have been blamed for affecting people's memory and ability to concentrate or make fast decisions – even though they feel more confident and able to make good decisions. They can also lead to clumsiness and shaky movements. The effects of some of the longer-lasting types continue into the following day.

Because of these various sedative effects, people who need to be wide awake and very alert, such as pilots, drivers and workers using complicated machinery, should not take tranquillizers. Indeed, their working conditions ban them from doing so.

'Sleepwalking'

When people use **benzodiazepines** for a long time, they may experience increasing feelings of tiredness, and have less energy. Some people have called this 'sleepwalking through life'.

Many drugs can affect alertness and skilled co-ordination, and should be avoided when operating machinery.

Very rarely, tranquillizers have the opposite effect to that intended, and increase anger and aggression.

Also, many benzodiazepine users find that they are less anxious but, as a side effect, they begin to feel more depressed. If they are prescribed **antidepressants** as well, the antidepressants themselves can have side effects. It rapidly becomes difficult to sort out the real problems and symptoms from the side effects of the different drugs.

In a small number of cases, tranquillizers can have the opposite effect to what is intended. They make people more restless, angry and aggressive. There is no way to predict if this will happen.

Robin's story

'It was great,' says Robin, a 31-year-old shopworker. 'For months I'd been feeling anxious. It began to affect my work. I was warned about my attitude and making too many mistakes. That made the problem worse and life at home became very tense. Finally I went to the doctor, and she prescribed a short course of tranquillizers. They worked, and the benefits began to affect my whole life. I could concentrate better. I spent more time dealing with what was happening, rather than worrying about what might happen. But I did feel myself slowing down and getting tired easily.'

After four weeks, the doctor advised Robin to stop taking the drug. Robin was concerned, but he managed to get over the event. He is now much happier, less nervous and more positive.

Tranquillizers and antidepressants

Many people think of tranquillizers and **antidepressants** as almost the same thing. They are pills that help to keep you calm, happy and relaxed. But they are quite different types of drugs, which work in different ways. Each type has its pros and cons.

Tranquillizers

As a summary, for comparison, tranquillizers are generally used to treat the symptoms of anxiety – feeling agitated, nervous and restless. They act relatively quickly to make people calmer, less nervous and more relaxed. Most work within a few hours and the effects wear off after a day or so. This means a person can take a tranquillizer now and again, as needed, to feel better when anxiety threatens. If feelings of anxiety fade, there may be no need to take another tablet for weeks. But tranquillizers are **sedatives**. They can make people feel drowsy and confused. If they are taken regularly, day after day, they can make life seem drab, colourless and flat.

In severe anxiety or during a 'panic attack', a person is extremely anxious. A casual thought or even a dream triggers a whole series of worries about what might happen.

28

Antidepressants

Tranquillizers can be dangerously addictive (see page 38). Antidepressants are less so. In recent years, more doctors have prescribed antidepressants, rather than tranquillizers, for anxiety. Some modern antidepressants are gradually taking over from older tranquillizers. Indeed, the distinction between the conditions of **depression** and anxiety is also becoming more and more blurred.

Antidepressants, as their name suggests, treat depression. This usually involves feelings of great sadness, despair and perhaps loneliness, when 'all seems lost'. There is often a lack of energy and little desire or motivation to be active and doing things. Antidepressant drugs do not 'cure' depression, but they can take away the symptoms.

In contrast to tranquillizers, most types of antidepressants do not take effect quickly. In fact, many take about three weeks to start working. Likewise, when they are stopped, it takes a long time for their effects to fade away. Modern antidepressants do not make people feel drowsy or sedated, as some tranquillizers do. But the antidepressant does not give a 'high' or a 'lift' either, with greatly raised mood and happiness. In fact, some people taking them notice hardly anything at all – except that they feel less depressed.

29

Tranquillizers as 'street' drugs

Many people experiment with 'street' drugs at some time in their lives. There are those who try them once or a few times, but then stop using them. Others continue to take them for social reasons, perhaps with groups of friends, or at a venue such as a club. These people are often called '**recreational users**'. In a few cases, people continue to use a drug and become **dependent** on it.

Heroin and its dangers

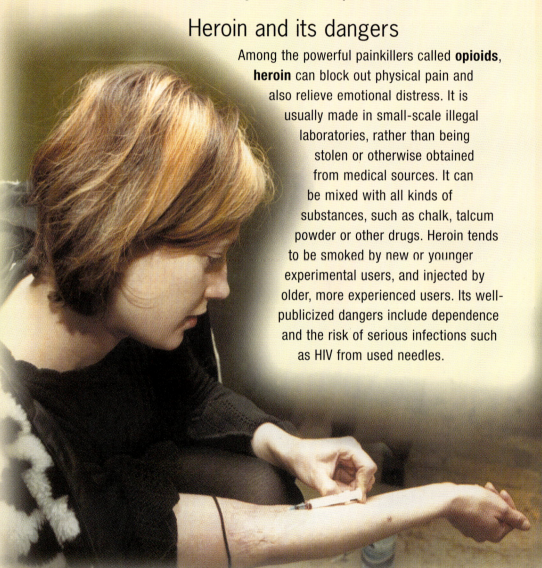

Among the powerful painkillers called **opioids**, **heroin** can block out physical pain and also relieve emotional distress. It is usually made in small-scale illegal laboratories, rather than being stolen or otherwise obtained from medical sources. It can be mixed with all kinds of substances, such as chalk, talcum powder or other drugs. Heroin tends to be smoked by new or younger experimental users, and injected by older, more experienced users. Its well-publicized dangers include dependence and the risk of serious infections such as HIV from used needles.

Misusing tranquillizers

Benzodiazepine tranquillizers became more common as street drugs in the 1980s. In some regions this partly resulted from shortages of heroin, due to less being made. Also, the police and other officials had increased success in seizing batches of the drug.

Temazepam was one of the most misused benzodiazepines, then diazepam (**Valium**) took its place. In 1998, 6 per cent of Australians used tranquillizers or sleeping pills for non-medical purposes.

Often these drugs are not taken alone, but with alcohol or opioids such as heroin, for a greater effect.

This young heroin user in Russia risks infection and drug dependence. When used as 'street' drugs, benzodiazepines have similar risks.

These combinations of drugs have led to an increase in substance abuse problems, because all three have a high risk of dependence. Drug-related deaths due to mixed tranquillizer-alcohol abuse have also risen in recent years.

On the street

On the street, medicinal drugs often have different names:

- Tranquillizers are known as 'benzos' or 'tranx'.
- Nitrazepam (**Mogadon**) tablets are 'moggies'.
- Temazepam pills are 'green eggs', 'jellies', 'jelly babies', 'rugby balls', 'tems' or 'yellow eggs'.

Rohypnol – the 'date rape' drug

The specialized tranquillizer flunitrazepam (Rohypnol) is known as a 'date rape' drug. Slipped unnoticed into a drink, it can cause sleepiness or blackout, and even short-term memory loss. The affected person is then at risk from rape or other abuse. There are severe penalties for illegally using or possessing this type of tranquillizer.

When drugs can be avoided

It is difficult to control or track the use of painkillers because the common types are so widely available as **over-the-counter** medicines. Undoubtedly, many people take painkillers and tranquillizers when they do not really need them. For example, even if the underlying reason for a person's pain has been cured, she or he may not want to stop the drug 'in case the pain comes back'. A few people even use painkillers to prevent pain in case of future accident, saying 'I might fall over and get hurt'. Such unnecessary drug use puts the body at needless risk of any **side effects**.

Therapies

Tranquillizers are usually obtained under a doctor's prescription. But first, the doctor will normally try to find the underlying reason for the anxiety. He or she may then be able to suggest alternatives for treatment, rather than prescribing pills for the anxiety itself. A patient could visit a counsellor or therapist, consider a change of lifestyle or try a **complementary** treatment such as relaxation therapy or **hypnotherapy**. Therapies such as **psychotherapy** are also available, through which problems are sorted out by talking about them and trying to understand them.

A short-term solution

However, in some cases, a short course of tranquillizers may be appropriate, usually as a last resort.

Medical guidelines state that **benzodiazepines** should be prescribed only for severe and disabling anxiety or insomnia (sleeplessness), which is causing unacceptable stress. These tranquillizers should not be used for mild anxiety. They should be prescribed only in small amounts, enough for two to four weeks.

Patients can help themselves by asking their doctor about the lowest dose that may be effective, and the shortest time the drug can be taken for. Also, when a course of tranquillizers is finished, patients can help themselves again. Is another course really needed? Can other changes be made to avoid the need for more drugs? If a patient feels there is no option but further tranquillizers, she or he is advised to see the doctor again, for another discussion, rather than simply ask for a repeat prescription.

Using drugs carefully

Drugs of any kind can be dangerous if used incorrectly. It is important to take any medicine exactly as recommended by the doctor or pharmacist, and never to take more than the stated dose. This is particularly important with painkillers, which can cause great harm if the dose is too high. Also, it is easy to become **dependent** on some types of tranquillizers.

Many non-drug methods have a relaxing and calming effect, such as having a massage with aromatic oils.

Dependence

A serious **side effect** of some drugs, including most tranquillizers and some painkillers, is **dependence**. This is often called 'getting hooked' or 'becoming addicted'. A person becomes so used to the drug, that they feel they have to carry on taking it. Perhaps they even believe they cannot live without it. The severity of the problem can vary from person to person. It is affected by the dose the individual is used to taking, and the length of time he or she has been using the drug.

Physical dependence

Dependence on a drug often has two aspects – physical and **psychological** (mental). Physical dependence occurs when the body has developed a chemical need for the drug. Without it, the body cannot carry on working as before. When the drug is stopped, this has effects on the body called **withdrawal symptoms**. Often these can be more unpleasant and more severe than the original problem that the drug was supposed to treat. Each type of drug creates its own range of withdrawal symptoms. They include aches and pains, muscle cramps, sweating, **nausea** (feeling sick) and uncontrollable shaking and crying.

Psychological dependence

Psychological dependence is based in the mind, in feelings and emotions. People believe that they must have the drug, or they will not be able to cope. There may be great sensations of pleasure, well-being and security from taking the drug, which will be shattered if the drug is stopped. The withdrawal symptoms often include **depression** and anxiety. In both physical and psychological dependence, there is a temptation to take 'just one more' pill of the drug, to ward off withdrawal symptoms. Another temptation is to take another drug in order to treat the withdrawal symptoms of the first.

Depression and lack of hope may occur both with dependence and withdrawal.

Drug tolerance

Drug **tolerance** occurs when the usual dose of the drug has less and less effect each time it is taken. To gain the same effect as before, the dose has to be increased. Tolerance can rise to a point where the amount of the drug is so high in each dose that it begins to have toxic (poisonous) effects on the body. This does not happen during normal use.

Dependence

Painkiller dependence

Most **over-the-counter** painkillers carry no risk of physical dependency. However, some people become dependent on painkillers that contain small amounts of the more powerful **opiate**-based painkiller, **codeine**. As described on page 17, codeine is often mixed with less powerful drugs, such as **paracetamol**, to make tablets that are sold as over-the-counter painkillers.

No warnings

There is no international agreement to put warnings about dependency on the packaging of painkillers with codeine or similar drugs. Surveys show that up to 8000 people in Britain could be affected. About 1.5 million Americans take prescription painkillers for non-medical reasons (1998). When they stop taking their tablets, they might not understand why they feel worse.

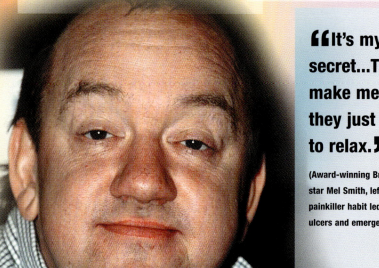

❝It's my dark secret...They didn't make me feel high – they just helped me to relax.❞

(Award-winning British comedian and film star Mel Smith, left, whose 50-tablets-a-day painkiller habit led to two burst stomach ulcers and emergency hospital treatment)

In a few cases, people who take very high doses of codeine-containing painkillers build up a chemical tolerance (see page 35). This means they have to take still more – up to 70 tablets a day – just to carry on feeling 'normal'. These painkillers are available only in limited quantities, to reduce the danger of **overdose**. The affected person feels driven to travel from one shop to another, just to get one day's supply.

Controlled painkillers

Powerful opiate-opioid painkillers can be legally used only under medical supervision, so that risks of dependence and tolerance can be assessed. But taken illegally, opiate drugs such as **heroin** and **morphine** can soon lead to both tolerance and dependence. It is possible for some people to live near-normal lives for many years while they are dependent on heroin. But hundreds die every year from accidental overdose, contaminated doses (with poisonous substances added), and infected needles and equipment. Thousands more go to prison, having turned to crime to obtain the money to pay for the drug.

Heroin withdrawal

Physical **withdrawal** from opiates-opioids such as heroin usually lasts about 10 days and is likened to severe 'flu with sweating, aches, pains, muscle spasms (painful tightening), sickness and stomach cramps (sudden muscle pain). Psychological dependence tends to last much longer. Ex-users often need support and counselling for months, as well as a change of surroundings and lifestyle, in order to 'kick the habit'.

Tranquillizer dependence

Dependence on **benzodiazepine** tranquillizers was a huge problem in the 1980s and 1990s, and is still an issue today. In Australia, for example, about 9 million benzodiazepine prescriptions are written each year. It has been called the 'third great addiction', after alcohol and the drug nicotine in tobacco. People take the amount of benzodiazepine they need to keep them going, just as nicotine users smoke a certain number of cigarettes everyday.

Getting hooked

It is impossible to become 'hooked' after taking just one benzodiazepine pill. But if these tranquillizers are taken regularly, the risk of dependence rises steeply after about two months. After a year, dependence is almost certain. The affected person carries on taking the same amount each day, perhaps for years. Yet the drug may have stopped working after only a few weeks. This is why benzodiazepine tranquillizers should not be taken for more than four weeks.

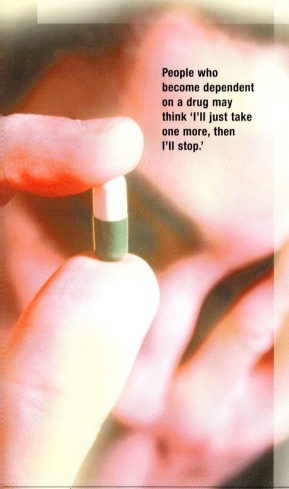

People who become dependent on a drug may think 'I'll just take one more, then I'll stop.'

Recognizing dependence

Dependence on benzodiazepines is quite common, but is not always easy to recognize or understand. Doctors look for signs such as loss of alertness, poor memory, being clumsy or accident-prone and, sometimes, aggressive behaviour. The ways that patients can recognize dependence in themselves are described on page 34.

Withdrawal symptoms

Withdrawal symptoms caused by suddenly stopping benzodiazepines can be as varied as they are severe. They include:

• aches and pains
• restlessness
• irregular heartbeat
• sweating
• loss of appetite
• feelings of pins-and-needles
• loss of muscle control with 'jelly legs' and 'the shakes'.

There may also be a return of the problems that the tranquillizer was originally supposed to treat, such as anxiety, restlessness, lack of sleep and panic attacks. It can be difficult to know if these problems are the effects of withdrawal, or the original symptoms coming back again.

Barbiturate dependence

Tolerance and dependence on **barbiturates** are serious problems, similar to those of 'hard' drugs such as heroin or cocaine. The problems are relatively rare today because barbiturates themselves are little used or misused.

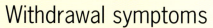

Dependence

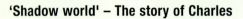

'Shadow world' – The story of Charles

The story of Charles shows the problems that heavy dependence on tranquillizers can cause. Charles was just 21 years old when he went to the doctor complaining that he felt tired and run-down. He felt he needed a 'pick-me-up'. This was 1964, just as benzodiazepine tranquillizers were becoming popular, but before their risks were understood. The doctor prescribed one of them.

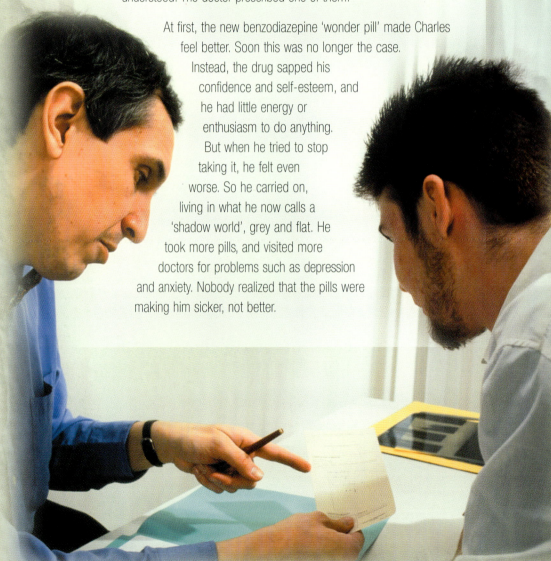

At first, the new benzodiazepine 'wonder pill' made Charles feel better. Soon this was no longer the case. Instead, the drug sapped his confidence and self-esteem, and he had little energy or enthusiasm to do anything. But when he tried to stop taking it, he felt even worse. So he carried on, living in what he now calls a 'shadow world', grey and flat. He took more pills, and visited more doctors for problems such as depression and anxiety. Nobody realized that the pills were making him sicker, not better.

Finally, in 1989, Charles's doctor stopped the pills – but suddenly, without warning or help. Charles suffered agonizing withdrawal symptoms that lasted for months. 'Nothing can prepare you for what I went through. I sat curled up on the settee, unable to move, with my heart rate racing through the roof. I couldn't walk, my vision was blurred, my skin was crawling. The worst thing was that I felt de-personalized, as if I was outside myself, looking in. I was terrified.'

Today, Charles feels normal again. But he regrets that he lost over 25 years of his life to the 'shadow world' brought on by benzodiazepine dependence. Today the problem is much better understood. People who have taken tranquillizers for a long time should be offered specialist help, to stop slowly and safely, without terrifying withdrawal symptoms.

❝At that time benzodiazepine was regarded as a panacea, a cure-all. I was told it would get me back on my feet. Nobody warned me about any side effects. What I really needed was a break, like a holiday. Instead I ended up becoming an addict.❞

(Charles today)

Stopping tranquillizers

There are no set rules about **dependence** on tranquillizers or other drugs, or about their **side effects** or **withdrawal symptoms**. Each person reacts differently. But in general, people who have been prescribed **benzodiazepine** tranquillizers for more than a month should seriously question both themselves, and the doctor, about why these drugs are still needed. The longer benzodiazepines are used, the greater the dependence and the harder it will be to stop, with more severe withdrawal symptoms.

A vicious circle

The first sign of trouble is often a feeling that the benzodiazepine drug is not working as it should. Indeed, this is probably true, since the body has got used to it and developed **tolerance**. Some of the original symptoms, such as anxiety and worry, difficulty in sleeping, and restlessness, might return. In addition, the person is likely to experience new feelings of irritability and tension. It may seem that the way to feel better is to take more of the drug. But this means tolerance and dependence increase, too. When this happens, the patient has entered a 'spiral of dependence' or a 'vicious circle'.

The decision to stop

If this happens, the patient has to make some clear decisions, with the aid of a doctor, and especially with a tranquillizer-dependency counsellor or someone else experienced in such problems. The patient must be certain that he or she wants to 'get off' the drug, because their life in the long term will be better without it. Once that decision has been firmly taken, the patient is helped to follow a series of carefully planned steps.

Stopping benzodiazepines

Suddenly stopping taking a benzodiazepine tranquillizer, after taking one regularly, can cause enormous problems. When the body is deprived of the drug abruptly, after months or years of use, the withdrawal symptoms can be extremely serious. They include severe confusion, **convulsions**, **hallucinations** and many other dangerous effects. Even for patients who have been taking the drug for only a short time, stopping suddenly can bring on 'rebound anxiety'. The feelings of worry and agitation are far worse than they originally were when the patient started taking tranquillizers.

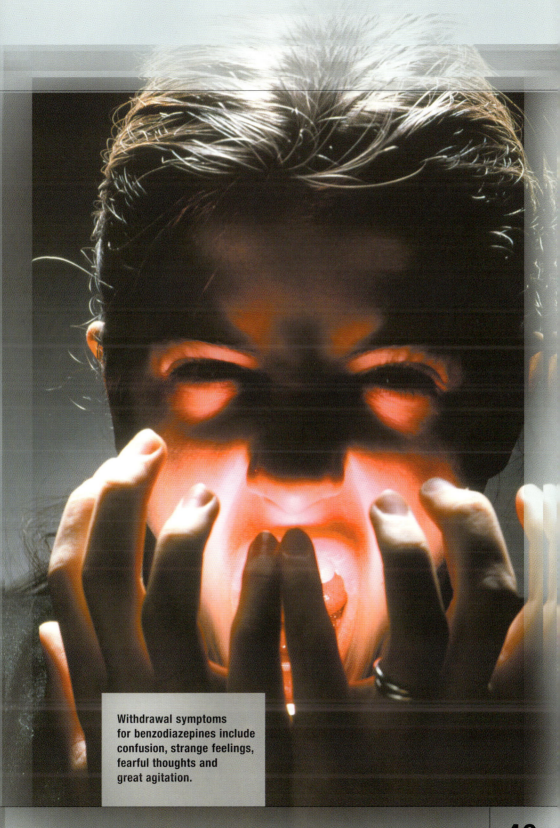

Withdrawal symptoms for benzodiazepines include confusion, strange feelings, fearful thoughts and great agitation.

Stopping tranquillizers

Anyone can stop taking benzodiazepine tranquillizers. But nobody who is dependent on them can expect to do it overnight. 'Coming off' a benzodiazepine tranquillizer must be done very slowly and carefully.

Tapering the dose

The main aim is to reduce gradually the amount of benzodiazepine tranquillizer taken, over a period of weeks or even months. This is called '**tapering**' the dose of the drug. In one form of tapering or **withdrawal** programme, the total daily dose of benzodiazepine is reduced by

about one-eighth. This reduced dose is kept constant as it is taken each day for two to three weeks. Then it is reduced again, by one-eighth of its new total, and taken for another two to three weeks, and so on.

Managing withdrawal

This form of withdrawal should be done with the help of a doctor and preferably an expert counsellor or adviser on benzodiazepine dependency. Some patients manage the programme largely by themselves, with background medical supervision. Others need plenty of advice and support. In general, the longer a patient has taken the drug, the more gradual the withdrawal should be. This also applies to people who have taken a benzodiazepine tranquillizer for another medical reason apart from anxiety, such as epilepsy.

Even during a very gradual 'taper', some patients with severe tranquillizer dependence can suffer withdrawal symptoms. If the drug is stopped too rapidly, these symptoms can include headaches, dizziness, nausea, **depression**, aching muscles, burning skin and even hallucinations.

Successful withdrawal

The speed and success of the withdrawal programme varies greatly. It depends on the variety of drug that the person has been taking, and for how long, and how seriously dependent he or she has become. As a general guide, it usually takes at least twelve weeks for a mildly dependent user to stop. A severely dependent long-term user will need over a year. The process of clearing a tranquillizer (or other drug) from the body is called **detoxification**. When it is complete, the person can expect to return to how he or she was before ever taking the drug.

❝Will my hands ever stop shaking like I have a terrible hangover? Will my brain be quiet, will my body be still, will I be able to say 'I'm happy to be alive' again? Will I believe life is worth living like I used to?❞

(Jen, recovering from benzodiazepine dependency, four months after stopping, from the online forum 'benzos')

Alternatives to drugs

There are many ways of coping with pain and anxiety that do not involve drugs. As with any health problem, it is advised to identify the basic cause first, and deal with that if possible. For example, a person with back pain could be sitting at a desk in a bad position, or lifting heavy loads using the wrong method. A person who is very anxious and restless might be studying an unsuitable course, or feeling crowded and cramped by family members at home. There are endless similar examples of how to solve the cause, rather than masking the symptoms with drugs. There are also approaches using therapies such as **psychotherapy** (see page 33).

Natural remedies

Many modern drugs have been developed from traditional natural remedies. Health shops and herbal suppliers stock a range of creams, tablets and lotions based on natural ingredients and plant extracts, for easing pain and calming anxiety. However, these remedies sometimes react with both prescribed and **over-the-counter** drugs. Not all are safe and effective in all cases. A pharmacist or qualified expert such as a herbalist can give proper advice.

Yoga, a relaxation technique for mind and body, is widely used to help cope with the stress of modern living.

Complementary therapy

Complementary medicines can be used in addition to **conventional medicine**. If the source of a pain is physical, such as poor posture, then a physical therapy such as manipulation, **osteopathy**, **chiropractic** or **Alexander Technique** may well assist. One of the most ancient therapies for relief of pain and anxiety is **acupuncture**. Yoga, meditation and **hypnotherapy** are other recognized techniques for relieving stress and quelling feelings of anxiety and worry.

Enjoying sport and exercise, especially with other people, can be a successful way of reducing anxiety and tension.

A healthy body

Another way to maintain a healthy and positive mind, and reduce anxiety, is to maintain a fit, healthy body. The best way is to do regular exercise, such as swimming, cycling, jogging, brisk walking or playing sports. Exercise and physical activity release natural body chemicals called **endorphins** in the brain. Endorphins have a role as the body's natural painkillers and they also increase feelings of well-being.

Legal matters

Tranquillizers and stronger painkillers are classed as **controlled drugs** (see right) in the UK, the USA, Australia and many other countries. It is against the law to possess these substances without a doctor's prescription. It is illegal to possess some types at all. The penalties are severe for those who are caught.

Possession of controlled drugs without a prescription can lead to a person being arrested.

Controlling drug use

In the UK, there are two main sets of laws relating to the availability of drugs. The Medicines Act 1968 concerns making and selling them. The Misuse of Drugs Act 1971 divides '**recreational**' drugs into groups, according to how dangerous they are. Drugs subject to the Misuse of Drugs Act are known as controlled drugs. Police and other authorities have special powers to stop and search people on 'reasonable suspicion' that they possess a controlled drug. In the USA, similar powers are provided by the Pure Food, Drug and Cosmetic Act (1938 plus amendments), which defines Prescription Required Drugs, and the Controlled Substances Act (1970).

The legal situation regarding drugs is complex. Simply giving one tablet to a friend may result in a prison sentence.

In addition to these national laws, many schools, colleges and similar organizations have their own sets of rules. Often these prevent the possession, use or sale of painkillers and other drugs on the premises. In some cases, even 'look-alike' pills are included (they look like real drugs, but don't contain active ingredients). It is part of the drive towards safer, drug-free surroundings. The only exceptions are people with medical conditions such as asthma, who have official permission for their drug treatments.

Minor tranquillizers

All minor tranquillizers, including the **benzodiazepine** group, are prescription-only medicines under the laws in the UK, the USA, Australia and many other countries. This means that they can be legally supplied on prescription only.

In many regions it is illegal to supply benzodiazepines to another person. Penalties for doing so can include fines or even prison. So if a person obtains tranquillizers with a doctor's prescription, and sells or gives some to another person, then he or she is committing an offence. For some tranquillizers, such as **temazepam** or flunitrazepam (Rohypnol), the controls are much stricter. Simply possessing them without a prescription is a serious offence. Similar strict controls and severe penalties apply to **barbiturate** tranquillizers.

People who can help

Despite many changes in prescribing guidelines, and publicity campaigns, **dependence** on **benzodiazepine** tranquillizers is still a relatively common problem today. In the UK, it is estimated that about 1 person in 50 could be affected. An estimated 4 million people in the USA have used prescribed benzodiazepines regularly for five years or more. A benzodiazepine-dependent person is advised to approach one of the official agencies or self-help groups for advice. Another starting point is to seek help more informally from a family member, a trusted friend, a member of a church or reputable religious group, or a trained counsellor. It is valuable to talk and listen, and take advice. The next stage is to move on to find some expert help, for guidance and support through the **withdrawal** process.

Self-help groups

Self-help groups for tranquillizer dependency exist in many countries. People can meet, share their concerns and get advice by phone, or over the Internet. Often the groups are run by people who have had experience of being dependent on benzodiazepines themselves. Similar groups also offer help for problems with dependency on common **over-the-counter** painkillers.

Starting points for beating benzodiazepine dependency

These types of sources provide details of local self-help groups, usually free of charge. Generally, the enquirer remains anonymous.
- GP (family doctor)
- local health or medical centre
- local library information lists
- trained counsellor in health and medical matters
- Citizen's Advice Bureau (UK)
- council information department (Australia)
- Medicare office, city hall or community centre (USA)
- Drug treatment services, substance abuse centres or detoxification centres, listed in phone books, libraries and on the Internet.

A list of national organizations that offer tranquillizer and painkiller withdrawal helplines is given on page 52. Most offer free advice over the phone, put people in touch with expert help, supply leaflets and videos, and perhaps arrange home visits.

Self-help sessions allow people to realize they are not alone, share their experiences, and receive first-hand advice about coping with drug dependence and withdrawal.

Future directions

Drug companies spend billions each year on researching new products, including new types of tranquillizers and painkillers. In many cases, tranquillizers are gradually being phased out, and replaced by **antidepressants**. Reseach into new painkillers includes the development of drugs called Cox-2 inhibitors. They also have anti-cancer effects, but in tests some types have been shown to affect the digestive system and liver, and the healing of wounds. Marijuana (cannabis), which is currently an illegal drug, has pain-relieving effects. Research is being carried out to find out whether the substances in it that have these effects can be made into safe prescription drugs.

Information and advice

Many organizations and pressure groups offer general information about drugs and how to cope with pain, anxiety and **depression**. Some organizations offer specific help with **withdrawal** from tranquillizers and **over-the-counter** painkillers. Contacts listed here can also provide information on organizations that provide help to cope with painful medical conditions such as back pain, arthritis and cancer.

Contacts in the UK

DRUG AWARENESS

British Association for Counselling and Psychotherapy (BACP)
1 Regent Place, Rugby CV21 2PJ
Tel: 0870 443 5252
www.bac.co.uk
The BACP has an extensive directory of counselling services relating to drugs and other issues throughout the UK. Enquiries are by post only. Enclose a stamped addressed envelope for a list of counsellors in your area.

Over-Count
9 Croft Road, Bankend Village,
Dumfries, DG1 4RW
Tel: 01387 770404
www.grieved.fsnet.co.uk
Drugs advice agency specializing in misuse or addiction to any over-the-counter, non-prescribed drug or medicine available at any UK pharmacist, including commonly used painkillers.

Release
388 Old Street, London EC1V 9LT
Helpline: 020 7729 9904
www.release.org.uk
Provides a range of services dedicated to meeting the health, welfare and legal needs of drug users, including people dependent on tranquillizers and those who live and work with them.

PAIN AWARENESS

Pain Concern
PO Box 13256, Haddington, EH41 4YD
Tel: 01620 822572
www.painconcern.org.uk
Self-help charity offering information and support for pain sufferers and their carers.

TRANQUILLIZERS

www.benzo.org.uk
Comprehensive website devoted to benzodiazepine addiction, withdrawal and recovery, including an email forum.

The Council for Involuntary Tranquillizer Addiction
Cavendish House, Brighton Road, Waterloo, Liverpool L22 5NG
Helpline: 0151 949 0102
www.liv.ac.uk/~csunit/community/cita.htm
Voluntary organization offering practical personal advice.

Contacts in the USA

American Pain Society
4700 W. Lake Ave, Glenview, IL 60025.
Tel: 847-375-4715
www.ampainsoc.org
An organization that aims to advance pain-related research, education, treatment and professional practice.

Center for Substance Abuse Prevention (CSAP)
1010 Wayne Avenue, Suite 850
Silver Spring, Maryland 20910
Tel: 301-459-1591 extension: 244
www.covesoft.com/csap.html
A federal programme to provide information and help communities to combat alcohol and drug problems.

National Chronic Pain Outreach Association
PO Box 274, Millboro, VA 24460-9606
Tel: 540-862-9437
A non-profit organization that offers a wide range of publications and audio tapes.

Contacts in Australia

Australian Pain Society
PO Box 571, Crows Nest, NSW 1585
Tel: 02 9954 4400
www.apsoc.org.au
A non-profit organization that aims to improve the treatment of pain by researching the causes and methods of alleviating it.

TRANX Australia
PO Box 186, Burwood, Melbourne, VIC 3125.
Tel: 03 9889 7355
www.tranx.org.au
Benzodiazepine withdrawal support through individual counselling, a telephone support and information service, and the preparation of resources to assist people recovering from tranquillizer dependency.

Further reading

Alex does Drugs, by Janine Amos; Cherrytree Books, 2002. A story of how a young person acquires and copes with a drug addiction.

Coping with Pain, **Coping with Headaches and Migraine, Coping with Back Pain, Feeling Good**, produced by Talking Life (Wendy Lloyd Audio Productions), in conjunction with the Pain Relief Foundation, Walton Hospital, Liverpool. Details from Talking Life, PO Box 1, Wirral, CH47 7DD Tel: 0151 632 0662 www.talkinglife.co.uk Available as Pain Management Packs (3 different pack options) or individually.

Drug Addict, by Suzie Haymon; Franklin Watts, 2002. Extended interviews with children and young adults who are drug addicts.

Drugs, by Sarah Lennard-Brown; Hodder Wayland, 2001. The dangers of drug addiction.

Drugs and You, by Bridget Lawless; Heinemann Library, 2000. This book includes case studies, facts and figures, tips and points of view.

How do Drink and Drugs Affect Me?, by Emma Haughton; Hodder Wayland, 1999. This title looks at the effect of drink and drugs on our physical and mental health, looking at alcohol, smoking, illegal drugs and medicinal drugs in depth.

Disclaimer
All the Internet addresses (URLs) given in this book were valid at the time of going to press. However, due to the dynamic nature of the Internet, some addresses may have changed, or sites may have changed or ceased to exist since publication. While the authors and Publisher regret any inconvenience this may cause readers, no responsibility for any such changes can be accepted by either the authors or the Publisher.

Glossary

acupuncture
ancient Eastern technique of pain relief and treatment for well-being, usually using needles placed into the skin

Alexander Technique
using posture and exercise, especially of the spine, to relieve illness and promote well-being

anaesthetics
substances that cause reduction or loss in sensation or feeling, including pain

analgesics
substances that lessen or reduce pain

antidepressants
drugs prescribed by doctors to treat depression

anti-inflammatories
substances that reduce inflammation (discomfort, redness, swelling, pain)

anxiolytics
substances that relieve anxiety

aspirin
widely used drug to relieve aches, pains, stiffness and inflammation

barbiturates
powerful tranquillizers rarely used nowadays

benzodiazepines
types of tranquillizers or anti-anxiety drugs, also used to treat sleeplessness

chiropractic
a treatment in which the spine is adjusted to help to cure health problems

codeine
pain-relieving drug with high dependence risk

complementary therapies
therapies used alongside conventional medicine to treat aspects of an illness that conventional medicine may not be able to deal with easily

controlled drugs
substances that are subject to laws, regulations or legal restrictions

conventional medicine
medicine practised by most doctors and hospitals in the Western world

convulsions
fits or seizures, when the body makes uncontrolled, often jerky movements

dependence
continuing need or desire for a substance, even when it no longer works

depression
feelings of extreme sadness, hopelessness, lack of energy, and feeling 'outside' of normal life

detoxification
ridding the body of a harmful or toxic substance

endorphins
natural substances in the body, which act in the nervous system and brain to reduce feelings of pain

hallucinations
something that seems real but is not, and is solely 'in the mind', including sights, sounds, smells, tastes, skin sensations and pains

heroin
powerful narcotic drug that relieves pain; it has many side effects and a high risk of dependency – medically it is referred to as diamorphine

hypnotherapy
a treatment involving sending the patient into a state of deep relaxation in which he or she can still see and hear and follow commands

hypnotics
substances that bring on feelings of drowsiness or altered consciousness (see also narcotics)

ibuprofen
widely used drug to relieve aches, pains, stiffness and inflammation

Librium
brand name for chlordiazepoxide, a benzodiazepine tranquillizer or anti-anxiety drug

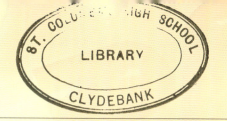
Mogadon
brand name for nitrazepam, a benzodiazepine tranquillizer or anti-anxiety drug used as a 'sleeping pill'

morphine
powerful narcotic drug that relieves pain; it also has many side effects and a high risk of dependency

narcotics
substances that bring on feelings of drowsiness or altered consciousness, and which may have risks of dependence (see also hypnotics)

nausea
feeling sick or about to throw up

nervous breakdown
common but misleading term for the time when a person cannot cope with daily life, due to an underlying problem such as a mental illness

NSAIDs
non-steroidal anti-inflammatory drugs, some of which are painkillers (include aspirin, ibuprofen and many others)

opiates-opioids
collective name for powerful narcotic drugs with a chemical make-up similar to substances such as morphine, originally derived from the opium poppy

opium
substance derived from the sweet sap (juice) of certain poppy plants, containing various substances that act as powerful narcotic drugs

osteopathy
the treatment of illness and pain by pressing and moving the bones and muscles

over-the-counter (OTC) drugs
substances that can be bought without a doctor's prescription

overdose
taking too much of a substance into the body, so that it has harmful or even deadly effects

paracetamol
widely used drug to relieve aches and pains, usually safe for babies and young people, but very dangerous in overdose

psychological
to do with human behaviour, the mind and mental activities

psychotherapy
treatments used for problems based in the mind rather than the physical body

recreational users
people who use drugs or substances occasionally, for non-medical purposes

sedative
increasing calmness and relaxation, generally slowing a person down

side effects
changes caused by a drug in the mind or body, which are not the intended effects, and which may be harmful

tapering
gradually reducing the dose of a drug

temazepam
benzodiazepine tranquillizer or anti-anxiety drug used as a 'sleeping pill'

tolerance
when the same amount of a drug gradually has less and less effect, so more and more of it is needed to maintain the original effect

Valium
brand name for diazepam, a benzodiazepine tranquillizer or anti-anxiety drug

withdrawal
stopping taking a drug

withdrawal symptoms
the effects, usually unpleasant, that occur when a drug is no longer taken; they may include sweating, muscle spasms, pains, sickness and hallucinations

Index

Titles in the *Need to Know* series include:

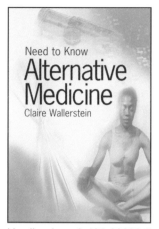

Hardback   0 431 09808 5

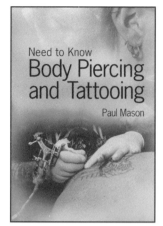

Hardback   0 431 09818 2

Hardback   0 431 09809 3

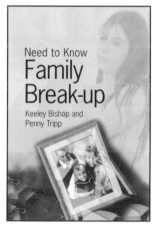

Hardback   0 431 09810 7

Hardback   0 431 09819 0

Hardback   0 431 09811 5

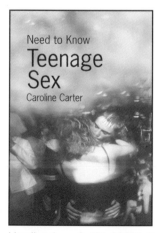

Hardback   0 431 09821 2

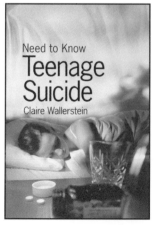

Hardback   0 431 09820 4

Find out about the other titles in this series on our website www.heinemann.co.uk/library